It's All About Time

"Understanding God's Creation"

I0180482

By:

WEDSON WITSON NYIRENDA

It's All About Time
"Understanding God's Creation"

By

Wedson Witson Nyirenda

Published By:

ABM Publications

A division of Andrew Bills Ministries Inc.

PO Box 6811, Orange, CA 92863

www.abmpublications.com

ISBN: 978-1-931820-69-1

TABLE OF CONTENTS

WEDSON WITSON NYIRENDA

ACKNOWLEDGEMENTS

I would like first of all to acknowledge the almighty God for His wisdom, strength and the Holy Spirit for inspiring me to put this book together. Without My God I wouldn't have written this book. I also would like to acknowledge the following men of God for their selfless efforts in making this project a success: My father in the Lord, Pastor Enoch Adejare Adeboye, the General Overseer of the Redeemed Christian Church of God, for his teachings. Daddy, your humility has really uplifted my soul and my zeal to do what God has always wanted me to do for His kingdom.

My spiritual father, Pastor Ayo Samuel Adeloye, the Special Assistant to the General Overseer of the Redeemed Christian Church of God- Southern Africa Region 1. Daddy you have been an encouragement in my life and your spiritual guidance has been the light in my life.

Pastor Emmanuel Lekan Olatoyinbo. You have been there for me and for my family in thick and thin. Thank you so very much for your prayers.

Evangelist, Dr. Charles Kazumba, for your inspiration, immeasurable support and encouragement you have given to me to publish this book, I say you are a God sent angel.

My Father, Mr Tenson Kambombo Nyirenda, your upbringing is a reason for all my successes in my life and my Mother, Etras Banda. Mum! you have taught me what a faithful child of God is supposed to be. You have gone through a lot and yet you still have a heart for those who wronged you. You are indeed a great woman of virtue.

Deacon Dabid Chilufya, my assistant Coach at Grupo Desportivo Hidroelectrica Cahora Bassa-Mozambique. Your support and loyalty amazes me. You are a dictionary of the Bible scriptures.

My dear wife Gillian, your Love for me is amazing, thank you for the support and encouragement you have always given to me; it is indeed a true reflection of what God meant when he said let us find a helper for man. My Children, Wedson Jr, Dorcas "Chichi", Melina, Mapalo and big boy Enoch for the love, understanding and support you have given to me. You are the source of my Strength and joy.

I would to acknowledge all my friends and family, thank you for your support over the years. You are all special people to me. May God bless you abundantly and may you never lack in your entire lives, in Jesus' name.

ENDORSEMENT

Brother Wedson Nyirenda is a passionate, dedicated and kingdom minded Servant of God whose life as a soccer coach, a former soccer star, life coach and a powerful minister of the Word of God is a blessing to this Generation and to the generation to come.

Reading this book by Deacon Nyirenda has indeed inspired me and built up my faith in Jesus Christ and revealed the mysteries of the knowledge of God through His word to me. After reading this book I can candidly say, I am not the same, the Spirit of God has transformed my thinking.

I highly therefore, endorse and recommend this book to any Christian, young and old who desire to grow in the Word and Power of God. I am confident that this book will inspire, build and establish you in the power of the word of God. The word and wisdom of God contained in this book no doubt has that power and ability to inspire you to know God in depth and to cause you to grow spiritually and in the ways of God.

I strongly encourage you as your brother in Christ to get this book and read it with a passion and see

God transform your character and nature right before your own eyes.

Evangelist, Dr. Kazumba Charles
Christ Passion Evangelistic Network
Saskatoon, Canada

<u>FOREWORD</u>

This book is a true testimony of what God can do to those who wait upon Him. The book can be used in academic teachings as well as theoretical teachings of the gospel of God. After reading this book, you will never be the same. There are so many mysteries that God is trying to reveal to His children but we have not been opening our eyes enough to dig out these mysteries.

This book is one of God's inspirations to reveal His treasures, which we have not seen all this while. When God wants to reach out to His own, He uses His servants, The Prophets, Pastors, Evangelists, Apostles, and so on. This is one of the ways The Almighty God has decided to reach out to you brethren and has specifically Hand packed you for His immeasurable blessings.

Get ready to have your life changed once and for all.

Deacon Wedson Witson Nyirenda

INTRODUCTION

There are two very powerful and influential factors, which determine our lives. The two factors are intertwined and co-exist. One of the two depends on the other in order to make human life easy and move. They are called **TIME AND MONEY.** God systematically created these two factors to make human life as well as He planned it to be before the creation of the universe. Time is the first born of the two. Time existed at the beginning and was these before God created the heavens and the earth.

Genesis 1:2, "And the earth was without form and void; and the darkness was upon the face of the deep. And the spirit of God moved upon the face of the waters". Here, it shows clearly that at this "time", God did not act to create what was already in his mind.

Genesis 1: 3-27; God began the creation of this whole universe from day one (1) (time), when he said let there be light, up to the day six (6) when he created the last but most important creature-man. What is the period between day one (1) and day six (6) called? "Time of Creation."

Time is a very important factor in our lives. And everything that exists now, either physically or spiritually must have existed before their creation, only in the eyes of the creator God.

EVIDENCE: Everything that is in existence now came from the first six days of creation of the universe. At the beginning God created original and authentic creatures and gave them command or rights to replicate and multiply.

Everything that God created within the six days of his work was "good." He saw that everything was perfect before releasing them into existence. That is why we say, "God is good, all the time, and all the time God is good. "Let me repeat this. Before God released anything into existence, He made certain that it was perfect.

Jeremiah 1:4-5, Then the word of God came unto me saying, Before I formed thee in the belly, I knew thee (everything about God is good) and before thou camest forth out of the womb I sanctified (separated) thee, and I ordained thee a prophet unto the nations.

This proves that everything that exists now must have been in existence before creation into the physical. In the eyes of God the creator everything He created in six days is good because everything about God is good—Therefore there is nothing under the sun that is not good. I repeat, "God is good all the time and all the time God is always good." You and I are not what we are supposed to be now. We were meant to be something better than what we are now.

Remember in the book of Genesis when bringing everything to existence; He saw everything and said," they were Good". In addition, as "Time" is running which he purposely put there, we are changing ourselves from our original design to something else.

Originally, His version and picture of what you and I were supposed to be was a perfect man, a ruler over all creation, and one with dominion over all creation. That is why you and I were created at last, specifically for us to come and enjoy everything already prepared for us by our Father, God. But it is important to understand that as "Time" is ticking or moving change is taking place in every created thing. Remember, I have just used the word "Originally". Between the "time "of original and "duplicate, there is "time running in transformation from the original state to the duplicated state.

In the book of **Genesis,** The original creation of human life (Adam and Eve) enjoyed all that was there to be enjoyed in the Garden of Eden. But as "time" passed by, the original creation (Adam and Eve) made a grave mistake that has brought problems to the duplicates that has come after them. "Running time of change."

Chapter 1

WHAT IS TIME?

According to the (Apple Dictionary), Time is defined as "the indefinite confirmed progress of existence in the past, present and the future regarded as the whole." I simply put it this way; "Time is the measure of periods. Let us look at the table below, which shows the different periods measured by "Time".

1.	MILLENIUM	-------	1000 YEARS
2.	CENTURY	-------	100 YEARS
3.	JUBILEE	-------	50 YEARS
4.	DECADE	-------	10 YEARS
5.	YEAR	-------	365 DAYS
6.	MONTH	-------	31/30/28 DAYS
7.	WEEK	-------	7 DAYS
8.	DAY	-------	24 HOURS
9.	HOUR	-------	60 MINUTES
10.	MINUTE	------	60 SECONDS
11.	SECOND	------	MILISECONDS

When we have a close look at the table above, we will find out that every particular period qualifies to another senior period after it reaches a stipulated "time." That is why for anything to come to its existence it must reach its given time. If you and I want to make something of any sort, we must take "time" to make that particular thing. If God Almighty, the creator of the whole universe took "time" of 6 days to create all His creation of His mind, what about you and I, the duplicate of Adam and Eve, who is the image of God?

Please look at the "Time" Chart above again; there is one thing I would like us to understand very clearly. Nothing that exists or created begins with the greatest "time", or in between that table. Everything that exists begins with the lowest period of time. And when we think critically, we find that the lower the period of time on that chart the faster the "time" runs. Everything that happens in our lives begins at zero (0), then one (1) and goes on. Have you come to think of why counting of numbers never begin from the greater numerals to lesser ones, why? This is simply because everything that exists must start from the lowest "time".

Can it be true now that everything about man is "time"? Is there any man/woman born already elder person from the womb of his/her mother? Do we celebrate our birthday because we have seen the coming days and years or we celebrate the past days and years we have seen? When one celebrates his birthday, he/she celebrate the "time" they have seen. In actual fact "A birthday is the mark of the period one has been in physical existence." But in real sense God has already seen the person's existence before he/she is formed in the mother's womb and knows where you are going.

WEDSON WITSON NYIRENDA

Chapter 2

PUZZLING QUESTION

If God is good all the time and all the time God is good, "Why do we have the poor, the rich, the wealthy, the sick, the so called unfortunate, bad hearted, the killers, the corrupt, the betrayers and the good people?

The answer to this question lies in Genesis 1:28-31. And God blessed them, and God said unto them, "be fruitful and multiply and replenish the earth, and subdue it; and have dominion over the fish of the sea and over the fowl of the air and over everything that moveth upon the earth. 29. And God said, behold I have given you every herb bearing seed, which is upon the face of all the earth and every tree in the which is the fruit of a tree yielding seed to you it shall be for meat. 30. And to every beast of the earth and every fowl of the air, and to everything that creepeth upon the earth, wherein there is life, I have given every herb for meat; and it was so. 31. And God saw everything that he had made and, behold, it was very good. And the evening and the morning (time) were the sixth day (time).

What do we make of these scriptures? God gave us the most powerful Right. The "Right of Choice of life." Therefore, man or woman has been given the right to choose the way he/she wants to live. And that is to live in abundance of God's blessings or chooses to live under the throne of Satan. To be a wealthy person or a poor person is a choice. To live a sickly or healthy life is a choice. To be corrupt or to be upright is a choice. To be the head or to be the tail is a choice.

All that man/woman transforms himself into from the "original plan" of God comes with the beginning of the count of "time" Remember at the count of zero (0), Adam and Eve were not in existence. A "time" came when they came into existence. That is the "time" when the creator decided that it was good "time" for them to exist. Then there came a "time" when Adam and Eve abused the "right of choice of living" and chose the other way which has affected all of us, the duplicates of Adam and Eve. By their (Adam and Eve) disobedience, we have found ourselves in the situation of dying.

I appeal to you today to be very careful with what we plan to do, or what we are doing, or what others are advising us, to be a part to this "time". Because a "time is definitely coming when the choice we have made or we are making, or what

IT'S ALL ABOUT TIME

we have done in "time", shall consequently affect us. Sometimes we may escape these choices and actions by passing on (dying). But don't think it is over. Because the duplicates (off springs) we leave behind, or the family relations remain to answer the questions when time comes. If we think by passing on (dying), we may escape the consequences then we have to think again. The greatest "Time" is coming with Judgment. The "time" We must face the creator who made you and I in the original form. Who after finishing His job in **Genesis** 1:31, inspected everything and at that "time" of your beginning said, "It is Good".

How would you and I answer when the creator ask us this question; "My dear………………………….. (Put your name in the dotted line). Are you as good or anywhere near the original plan I made you to be?"

If God created man/woman in His image and in His likeness He created both of them, it means that He duplicated Himself into someone at a "time "He deemed fit and when and when He gave man/woman the right of choice to life, He wanted to sit back and rest and watch His product function in a greatest manner He really imagined and saw should be. That is why He took "time" to perfect the creation and at last certified, "It was good."

When we say, "God is good all the "time" and all the "time" God is good; We mean to say, "We are supposed to be good all the "time" and all the "time" we are supposed to be good, because we are the image of God. Everything about God and in God is good.

When you sow a seed of hatred, deceit, corruption, murder, gossip, betrayal, mockery, be assured that in God's "time" you will receive a bountiful of the same harvest. If the "time" of harvest for your handwork comes after you have died, be assured that your duplicates will be there to harvest from your handwork. ADAM and EVE are not here, but we are reaping from their seed of disobedience, which is death.

Chapter 3

HERE IS A STORY

A man cultivated and planted maize (time) on a fifty (50) hectare of land. After the weeding season (Time), the maize grew nicely. According to the farm manager's projection, they were to harvest about fifteen (15) thousand bags of maize.

The owner of the farm was so glad because the **"time and money"** he had invested in was finally going to pay. But as fate could be; the man died a month before the harvest.

It was a sad situation for the family. But when "God's time" of harvest finally came, the family was happy again because the 'originator of the plan' and project, the seed sower, had done a good job for them before he passed on and they lived to enjoy from the "time" he took to sow the seed, weeding and nurturing.

Do we take time to think about how the plans and actions we do this "time" will affect our duplicates, family members and relations in a "time to come"?

EXERCISE:

Think as far back as one (1) year, or six (6) months, or even a month. And write down what has come out of anything you may have done, whether good or bad.

If nothing has yet come through, be assured that it is coming.

1. Write down—one (1) or two good things you did in the past one (1) year

_____

_____

_____

_____

_____

What was the result of it?

_____

_____

_____

_____

_____

2. Write down —one (1) or two (2) bad things you did in the past one (1) year.

_____

_____

_____

_____

_____

_____

_____

What was the result of it?

_____

_____

_____

_____

ANOTHER STORY

When I was doing my secondary School Education at Chingola High School in Chingola, I had a very good friend who was also a very good football player (Soccer). He was at a different high school than me but we lived in the same town. This brother was very intelligent in school. But he had a habit of 'petty thieving.' When I discovered that he was the one behind all the things we were missing in camp (Football camp), I spoke to him in strongest terms as team captain, but he answered me that I should mind my own business because the things he was stealing were not mine but for the company. So I decided to leave him alone and mind my own business at that "time." He left Chingola town and joined a club in Lusaka (the capital city of Zambia). The club employed him as a stores man. He was living good and decent life as the company he was working for looked after him and his family very well.

As "time" could be; the habit of stealing manifested into something uncontrollable. He was fired from work for stealing two (2) packets of 2kg sugar. To cut the story short, by this "time" my dear friend has no job, his wife left him, his children are suffering. He begs from one person to another.

Chapter 4

What Is Time and What Do You Understand About It?

You are about to find out the shock of your life today about what and who "TIME" is: They say "time" is everything. WHY? Because "time is "JESUS."

JESUS THE ANCIENT OF TIMES

HEBREWS 13: 8 "JESUS CHRIST THE SAME YESTERDAY, TODAY AND FOREVER" (This is exactly how the word "time" is defined in the Apple Dictionary): "The indefinite confirmed progress of existence in the past, present and future regarded as the whole."

Jesus is time, you waste time you lose, and you respect time you win. The more "time' you spend on Godly things, the more prosperous you become. The more time you spend on ungodly things, you lose big time. When you spend "time" on unproductive things, you drag yourself into poverty. Unproductive things are things like gossip, lies, betrayal, murder, laziness etc.

When we talk of the existence of anything

including heavens and earth, we talk of "time". When was it there? Is it there? Will it be there? All this talk of "time of existence. If Jesus is the same yesterday, today and forever, what are we talking about? We are talking about "time" Check the way you spend every minute of your life.

EXERCISE:

A day consists of twelve (12) hours daytime and twelve (12) hours nighttime.

1. How productive are you in the twelve (12) hours God has given to you for the daytime?

_____

_____

_____

_____

_____

_____

_____

_____

2. How productive are you in the twelve (12) hours God has given to you for the nighttime?

_____

_____

_____

_____

_____

_____

_____

_____

3. How many hours do you work in a day to get what you want?

_____

_____

_____

_____

_____

_____

_____

4. How much have you achieved from the hours you use per day?

_____

_____

_____

_____

_____

_____

_____

_____

5. Are you satisfied with what you have achieved and how you are living?

_____

_____

_____

_____

_____

_____

_____

6. Do you think if God increased the day to consist of eighteen (18) hours daytime and eighteen (18) hours nighttime, you would benefit more or it will still be sheer waste of "time"? (JESUS CHRIST). *That is why when God saw that things were not going the way he planned, He sent to us more of our time (JESUS CHRIST) in form of human being to come and correct everything.*

_____

_____

_____

_____

_____

_____

_____

_____

_____

_____

_____

7. Try to make your daily routine program just for one (1) day.

_____

_____

_____

_____

_____

_____

_____

_____

GENESIS 1:26, And God said, "Let us make man in our image, after our likeness; and let them (all of us) have dominion over the fish of the sea, and over the fowl of the air, and over the cattle and over all the earth (creation=time) **"US"** Means God, Jesus and the Holy Spirit.

Jesus was there before and during the creation of everything (time). When God entrusted Adam and Eve with the care of the precious garden, Jesus was there. "JESUS CHRIST, THE SAME YESTREDAY, TODAY AND FOREVER."

All the genuinely wealthy persons in this world are connected to "good use of time (Jesus Christ). Some have used their time (Jesus Christ) well at school and now they are living big. But some think they are the ones who have done it for themselves. The truth is that the "time" (Jesus Christ) one is studying and working on their studies is considered "good". Go back to Genesis 1:31. And God saw everything that he had made, and, behold it was very "Good".

TIME =GOOD=JESUS CHRIST

GOOD=TIME=JESUS CHRIST

Chapter 5

TIME IS THE HEALER, SO THE SAYING GOES

Every wound is healed with time. As time passes by the wound heals.

Every sickness heals with time. As time passes by the sickness heals.

Every broken heart heals with time. As time passes by, the heartbreak is mended.

Every serious problem ends with time. As time passes by the problems disappear.

Every wound and sickness called by name bows down to the highest name called JESUS CHRIST, who is the "time". Because He is time, everything heals with Him.

MARK 7:33-35, *after he took him aside, away from the crowd, Jesus put his fingers into the man's ears. Then he spit and touched the man's tongue. He looked up to heaven and with a deep sigh said to him, "Ephpatha!"(Which means, "Be opened!"). At this, the man's ears were opened; his tongue was loosened and began to speak plainly.*

This is clear testimony and evidence that only when your "time" arrives shall you be healed from your ailment. When you call upon Jesus, you are simply calling upon your time to come and pass. Every broken heart gets mended with time (Jesus Christ).

Sara the wife of Abraham lived most of her life broken hearted due to not having a child of her own. She gave up on the idea of having a child due to her age. She had crossed over her menopause stage. But because she and her husband Abraham were so faithful to God the Father, their "time" came to pass by them.

GENESIS 21: 1- 2, *Now the Lord was gracious to Sarah as he had said, and the Lord did for Sarah what he had promised. Sarah became pregnant and bore a son to Abraham in his old age; at the very "time" God had promised him.*

What then shall we say about the Sabbath?

A Sabbath is a day. A day is "time". Time is Jesus. No Jesus No Time, No Time No Sabbath.

MARK 2: 23- 28, *One Sabbath Jesus was going through the grainfields, and as his disciples walked along, they began to pick some heads of grain. The Pharisees said to him, "Look, why are they doing what is unlawful on the Sabbath?"*

He answered, "Have you never read what David did when he and his companion were hungry and in need? In the days of Abiathar the high priest, he entered the house of God and ate consecrated bread, which is lawful only for priests to eat. And he also gave some to his companions." Then he said to them, "The Sabbath was made for man, not man for Sabbath. 28- So the son of man is Lord even of the Sabbath.

Jesus is everything. He is also the Sabbath itself. The Sabbath is the Day, the Day is Time and the Time is JESUS CHRIST THE LORD.

MARK 3: 3 -5, *Jesus said to the man with the shriveled hand, "Stand up in front of everyone." Then Jesus asked them, "Which is Lawful on the Sabbath: to do good or to do evil, to save life or to kill?" But they remained silent. He looked around at them in anger and deeply distressed at their stubborn hearts, said to the man, "Stretch out your hand." He stretched it out, and his hand was completely restored.*

What was Jesus trying to reveal here? He was trying to make them realize that He was the Law and the Sabbath himself. That is why he also went on to remind the people that it was only right to do Good and not Evil in his Name. It was only right to save a life and not kill in his name. The Sabbath being a day is "Time," And as we have already learnt earlier, "Time" is Jesus.

Worship and praise your God every time. This is to say that each time you are praying, praising or worshipping God you must mention Jesus Christ because he is the Way and the truth. No one gets to His Father except through Him. Therefore, he who respects "time" shall never want in life.

Have you ever seen or heard of anyone selling time? The answer is obvious NO. No One has ever sold time in our time, but I know someone who has.

Let's turn to the book of Matthew 26:14-15, "*Then one of the twelve disciples called Judas Iscariot, went unto the chief priests. And said unto them, "What will you give me, and I will deliver him (Jesus-time) unto you? And they covenanted with him for thirty (30) pieces of silver (money)."*

In our lifetime there are some people who have "sold" others out (betrayed). And there are those engaging in human trafficking for money. When you betray or sell others out, you are simply selling Jesus out. Because man was made in God's image and in His image He created all of us. If all were made in God's image that is also Jesus Christ then you are selling out or betraying God, Jesus and the Holy Spirit.

1 Timothy 6-10- *"For the love of money is the root cause of all evil; which while some coveted after they have erred from the faith and pierced themselves through with many sorrows."*

Matthew 27:3-5, *"Judas which had betrayed Him, When he saw that he was condemned, repented himself and brought again the thirty (30) pieces of silver (money) to the chief priests and elders. Saying, I have sinned in that I betrayed the innocent blood. And they said, what is that to us? See thou to that. And he cast down the pieces of silver (money) in the temple and departed and went and hanged himself."*

Chapter 6

MONEY

Long time ago, people used to trade by exchanging goods for goods. This was called "Barter" system. But as "time" (Jesus Christ) weighed and measured this system "Time," (Jesus Christ) decided to say "No you cannot trade like this in my presence (time). You must find one measurement that will be used as a medium of exchange. He gave someone the notion and knowledge of inventing a medium of exchange called money.

But I "time" must warn you that this money must just be a medium of exchange for goods and services, not for exchange of man or life. (1 Timothy 6:10)

When you need spices you must produce this medium (money) then get your spices. If you need more of the "money" you must spend more of your "time"(Jesus Christ) to make it and go and use to get what you need (good- Genesis 1:31). Which were also produced using "time" (Jesus Christ) Because He was there when all were created, and given to man (His image and likeness).

WHAT IS MONEY?

There are several definitions for money, but for now we are going to look at three (3) for our lessons:

a. They say money is the current medium of exchange in the form of coins and notes.
b. Or, the assets, property and resources owned by someone or something; WEALTH;
c. Payment for work; wages (This is according to Apple dictionary)

My definition:

"Money is the medium of exchange for one's "time" spent on discovering, making or doing something." The value or worth of anything is determined by how much price in terms of "money" is pegged on the item. If this is the case, then "money" also describes how much "time" (Jesus Christ) one spent or took in planning, creating and making the product on display. (How much Jesus was involved in your work). The more "time" (Jesus Christ) is taken in planning, creativity and making anything, the more valuable the product is. Therefore, the price in terms of money for the product in question becomes higher.

EXAMPLE (Case study)

If one man is employed to do a job for eight (8) hours a day for five (5) days to produce one product and he is paid $100.00 for the job—This means that the man spends forty (40) hours in five (5) days (time) to make $100.00 (money) for himself.

If this man wants to make $400.00 (money), how much "time" or days must he be prepared to do before he gets the $400.00?

USD 100.00----40HRS (8 DAYS MULTIPLY BY 5 DAYS)

USD 400.00 ------------?

400/ 100 OF 40 = 160HRS

Days--- 160hrs/ 8hrs = 20 days.

For this man to earn USD 400.00 he must be ready to increase his working "time" from 40hrs (8days) to 160hrs (20) days. The more "time" you spend with your God (Jesus Christ) the more money – wealth comes your way. When I said that "Time and money are a pair and they are intertwined; this is what I meant. Money depends on "Time" (JESUS CHRIST). If you don't want to spend your time wisely and productively, forget about having money that you need. The wiser and productive you become with the way you use "time" (JESUS CHRIST), the more money (wealthy) you get out of it.

Money calls "time" and "time" calls money." Most people spend their precious "time" on things, which are unprofitable. Some would spend more than six (6) hours in a bar or club wasting their hard earned cash all in the name of 'interaction", while their families at home have nothing to eat.

TIME IS MONEY!

I Have Heard Of This Saying Uncountable Times; Have You? Without spending your "time" on anything, you can't get the money you need. And be assured of not having all the necessities you require. Let us ask ourselves if where we are, what we are doing is worth the time you spending. There are so many ways of making money react to "time".

TWO TYPES OF JOBS

There are two types of jobs in this world.
The first job is the job where one uses his time, strength and efforts and at the end of it all, he/she is the one paying the employer.
For instance, when you work so hard and earn some money and you decide that you shall be patronizing Beer parlors to spend your money.

Then know that you have just succeeded in getting employed by Beer parlor owners where when you god to work yourself up by drinking their beer, at the end of it all you will have paid them your hard earned money. In such cases many families have suffered and marriages broken.

The second job is the one where one goes to work, suffers for his hard earned money and takes his dues at the end of the job. If well spent, that money will multiply and grow into its own boss which in turn will employ others to do the jobs for him/her while he/she just controls things.

INVISIBLE PROPERTIES:

Some people spend most of their "time" thinking, planning and creating ideas of how to produce something that will make impact in life. If you look at the definition of money I earlier gave in the chapters before, you will see that money can be considered to be a "property". Hence, one's "time" of thinking, planning and creativity of ideas; is the 'property' that one puts on the shelf to attract "money" (Time Is Money). In this case, one possesses "time" in form of **'invisible property'.** In Addition, such kind of property is so expensive than the visible (physical) ones. There are laws that protect the rights of the owners of such properties in the world. For someone else to use someone's 'property (ideas) he/she must pay so much "money" for copyright or use of someone's "time" (Jesus Christ) of thinking, planning and creativity. This way of using "time" is so taxing in terms of thinking, but it pays handsomely. Who says it is easy to be a Christian anyway?

The types of works in this category are:

(a) Innovation (scientific)
(b) Architecture
(c) Computer science designing
(d) Medical science
(e) Teaching at high level education
(f) Fashion designing
(g) Motivation speaking
(h) Psychology

Men or women in this category depend largely on their brains. Once they complete their works (time), they sit back and wait for their "money to start coming through.

Examples: The legendary Computer designer (late) Mr. Stephen Job. He has left his Properties (time he spent) still multiplying money even when he has long gone to rest. Apple products are so valuable in the range of computers and they are so expensive in terms of price because the makers took good "time" to think, plan and later create their products with precision.

Bill Gates, Chief of Microsoft did his work long time ago and now he is sitting down just improving on his works. This is now his "time" to look at what is coming in terms of returns (money). He has been so humane to this world by assisting in many situations, ranging from poverty to health.

VISIBLE PROPERTIES:

Visible Properties are works that are physically seen, for example things such as labor. One can spend "time" doing his job physically in order to attract the money. In this category, thinking is not so much. Thinking is over shadowed by physical strength. The disadvantage of depending on your physical strength is that; one can't do the job for too long due to exhaustion. You get worn out easily. (That is typically why Football or any other physical sports are known to be "short term careers. It must be noted that in the game of football, there are both too much of quick thinking at very quick time while using physical strength")

We usually advise our players to work hard and save their money well because when the strength runs out, they could have accumulated enough to lean on. This is equivalent to spending their time wisely while they still have it.

DIFFERENT WAYS OF ACCUMULATING WEALTH (MONEY)

1. Wrong ways of using your "time" (Jesus Christ):

- By stealing from your employers, conning others, murdering people, and betraying or selling out others in exchange of money, you are just wasting and misusing your precious "time".
- Using of charms (Juju) to accumulate wealth.
- By stealing from your employers, you are not using your "time" (Jesus Christ), the way God designed you to be.
- By conning others out of their hard earned time and money, you are not using your God-given "time" (Jesus Christ) appropriately.
- By murdering others for money you are contaminating your "time" (Jesus Christ) with blood.
- By betraying or selling out others for money, you are just bringing your "time" (Jesus Christ) to a halt.

- By using charms (Juju) to accumulate wealth; Oh yes it seems so quick and shortcut, but as you practice all those fetishes and filthy practices remember that you are doing it in the presence of "time" (Jesus Christ) and He can't live in that filthy environment; therefore, He will at one "time" bring you to light and expose you Remember He said he is the "light" of this world. That is why they say, "Truth never dies no matter how long it may take, why? Because the "Truth is time." And Jesus is truth and time. "JESUS THE SAME YESTERDAY, TODAY AND FOREVER. Nothing can hide under the sun.

Money has never been and will never be evil. But its love is the root cause of evil because of our selfishness. The right of choice to live our lives the way we want has always turned us from the original humans we were meant to be, to the different creatures resembling man. Because of money people have been changed to different animals.

TESTIMONY:

My father in the Lord, Pastor Enoch Adejare Adeboye, the General Overseer of The Redeemed

Christian Church of God, once told us a story of a man who was very rich. This man had everything that money could buy. But it was the way he accumulated his wealth that was not acceptable.

His family was living like queens and kings, but they never knew how this man was being tormented by the covenant he entered into.

Every night before supper, the man would sneak out of the house, walk down the road to where he could find the rubble of rubbish piled by the side of the road. He would eat rotten food from there and clean his mouth and walk back home quickly in time for supper with his family.

One day as my father in the Lord was praying this man received Christ and got delivered from the captivity of Satan. He had been spending his "time" (Jesus Christ) wrongly.

THE MOST POWERFUL AND INFLUENTIAL PAIR (TIME AND MONEY) HAS BROUGHT ABOUT THE CREATION OF FOUR (4) TYPES OF PEOPLE IN THE WORLD:

	TIME	MONEY
PERSON 1	YES	NO
PERSON 2	NO	YES
PERSON 3	NO	NO
PERSON 4	YES	YES

THE BIG QUESTION IS: Where do you belong?

PERSON 1.

The persons in this group are those who have all the "time" in this world, but they have no money.

WHY? If "time" is Jesus Christ,

- They have the "time" but do not use it well.
- They use most of their time on useless things unproductive things e.g. Gossip, rumor mongering, backbiting (Remember backbiters are always at the back of those they backbite; that is why they are called backbiters)
- They use their abundant "time" (Jesus) on ungodly things. Jesus is tormented in them and cannot manifest the blessings He has for them.

- They use their "time" to confess negativity in their lives. Jesus Christ (time) in them cannot help because they keep on confessing the opposite of who Jesus is "Greater than he who is out there."
- They have all it takes to accumulate wealth but they can't see. For instance, there are so many people who are so talented but they have ended up dying in abject poverty. They have (Jesus Christ) who is Greater than that which is in the world; meaning all talents deposited in them are put to waste.

PERSON 2.

There are people who have "NO TIME" (Jesus Christ) but they have money. The question is How come?

- This group of people is so common in our society now. These men/women don't mind or care how and what they do in order to get the wealth they have.
- They don't have respect for "time" (Jesus Christ) as long as they have money. Money comes through dubiously, but it is just the matter of "time" (Jesus Christ) before they fall into the ditch.

- They have accumulated the wealth they have from stealing, betrayal, killing, charms etc.
- They don't see no wrong in whatever they do with their "time" Even the way they spend the money they have no regard for "time" or anyone. Therefore their fall is eminent and when it comes it is a heavy fall.
- They have many unwanted affairs. (Adultery, Fornication, prostitution)
- They don't have many genuine friends for fear of being exposed.
- Because they don't have many friends, they are so insecure. (No Jesus in them)
- Not having "time" is not having Jesus Christ. They worship money and other idols than anything else. (If Jesus is the ancient of time and was with God during the of this universe, then having money without Jesus is in vain)
- When Jesus "time" says enough is enough, then the person in-group 2 falls further to group 3.
- Most of the people who fall from group 2 to group 3 live very miserable lives. At this "time" it would have become very difficult to get back to group 1 where they can repent and change because of too much

shame. (Remember in-group 1 that is where we find gossipers rumormongers and backbiters. So for one to get back to that category, they fear. Hence choose to be isolated and die in a miserable way).

- It takes a very strong character, brave heart and mind to get back to group 1.

- By this "time" they could have learnt the hard way. When they get back to group 1, they change the way they use "time"-Jesus, (this is when we see some becoming born again. And in no time they start recovering and wealth start flowing their way. If they maintain the respect for and use of" time"(Jesus Christ) the wisdom of using money manifests and they find themselves in the "ELITE GROUP 4.

PERSON 3:

These are the worst kind of people and live the worst kind of life one could ever think of. These people have "NO TIME" and don't have money.

- I call the people in this group "the walking dead". Reason being that at this time one has succeeded in chasing away "time" (Jesus Christ) and at the same time money cannot come.

- They have no time to think or work (no time-no money).
- The only thing they think of is to beg for anything starting from food, clothes shelter, you can name it all.
- They multiply their woes by soaking themselves in alcohol thinking that problems will leave them. And yet that is when they push themselves into the deepest end.
- When you ask them about "time" they don't know. They can't even differentiate between day and night.

PERSON 4:
True riches and wealth are found with the people in this category.

- They respect "time" and the accumulate genuine wealth and money.
- They don't stop thinking, planning creating and innovating. Therefore money keeps flowing.
- When they create something or succeed in one area or thing, they do not go to sleep. They start thinking even the more (time) about what they have achieved and think of ways on how to improve their product.

- Time (Jesus Christ) multiplies their wealth the more.
- Having time (Jesus Christ) is worshipping Him, paying tithes, and offering, cheerfully giving to the poor and needy. In turn Jesus (time) manifests in great multiplication of wealth, sound health, all sorts of favor to the overflow.
- These people live in abundance and do not lack.
- Because they have all the "time" (Jesus Christ) in their life, Money and wealth start to work for them such that they never have to work themselves like slaves again. Because the one in them is greater than that which is in the world.
- He who is in them (time –Jesus Christ) starts to push the wealth to the overflow.
- Because they have "time" (Jesus Christ) and money, they can now sit back in their old age and rest. They only thing they do are to fight for where to go for holidays with the family members.

QUESTION AGAIN; WHERE DO YOU BELONG?

1. If you are in category 1, do you think you can change and move to group 4? If so, what areas

do you think are you weaknesses that you should work on in order to change?

_____

_____

_____

_____

_____

2. How much time do you think this would take you in order to get to the "Elite group 4, considering your age?

_____

_____

_____

_____

_____

3. If you are forty years and above, don't despair, remember Luke 1:37 "NOTHING IS IMPOSSIBLE WITH GOD".

_____

_____

_____

_____

_____

If you are in category 2, I urge you to repent all your sins. Confess all you have done and restitute before it is too late.

- Don't let it get too late that you fall into category 3.
- I must say you are in danger because one step further and you are going to the unpleasant stage.

If you are in Group 3 already,
- I must say that your case is a very delicate and difficulty one. I pray that God in His infinite mercies will forgive you and restore you. Take a huge step and do the right thing. Know Jesus and "time" will accept you then you shall see peace again. Only Jesus can restore you.

If you are in category 4. **_HALLELUYAH!!!_** Praise the Lord you are a true duplicate of your daddy – GOD, JESUS AND HOLY SPIRIT IS AT WORK.
Now that we have come to understand the true meaning of "time", what is it going to be like? Are

you going to continue living in the past where you don't regard time?

My brothers and sisters I encourage you to make a change to your life today and see how treasures of God's kingdom are unearthed. Change for the better and turn your family generation into a great example to others.

WEDSON WITSON NYIRENDA

Chapter 7

CHANGE

WHAT IS CHANGE?
Change is the moving from one form or state to the other. There are two main types of change in this life we live in. The first type is when there is change from a negative form or state to the positive one. The other change is when there is change from the positive form or state to the negative state.

CHANGING FROM NEGATIVE TO POSITIVE STATE:
Many have changed from evil to righteousness. To make such change is not easy. One has to make a very brave decision to move away from the things he or she has been enjoying doing in the past. To be honest, the evil things look more attractive and better than the righteous things. In truth the evil things are not as pretty as they appear. They conceal so much suffering inside of them.

That is why it is not as easy as it seems to follow Jesus and be his rightful disciple. This is because to a natural eye, Christianity looks to be boring.

When one makes this decision, he must be ready to lose all that was glittering in his life and take the ones which look not so shiny but rich inside.

CHANGING FROM POSITIVE TO NEGATIVE STATE:
This type of change is so easy. To stop doing Good and start doing evil is so easy. It does not even take much of one's time. As already alluded to Evil is very attractive while Good looks dull. Evil calls loud while Good whispers. It takes a very strong and faithful heart to withstand the pressure of Evil when it visits someone.

When you are Christ's follower, it is so easy for you to fall than even the way you stood up and accepted him. I have come to understand why Peter who was the closest disciple of the Lord Jesus Christ was the one who denied the Lord Three times. Many of us hear about this and laugh saying we could have done better. But we are worse than Peter himself, because each day that passes in our lives we deny the Lord as many times as possibly can.

The other example of changing from Positive to negative is when one is wealthy and drops down to a common poor person. In this situation also it takes a very strong heart, faithful and disciplined person to sustain the status quo. By the twinkle of an eye one can find himself begging from a wealthy status.

TO BE ASSURED OF POSITIVE CHANGE:
One must only be in Christ to be assured of positive change and live in it forever. Why then should we accept that only living in Christ will give us the peace of mind that we are looking for every day and night? They say "CHANGE is the only thing which is CONSTANT in life." CONSTANT means that something or someone is SAME all times. From inception till the end of time this thing or person is the same. To prove that only in Christ shall we find POSITIVE CHANGE, let us go back to our Bible reading in the book of HEBREWS 13: 8 which says, "Jesus Christ is the same Yesterday and Today and forever. This scripture confirms that only in Christ Jesus can one make a meaningful and right change.

Let us see an example of a marriage. A marriage not founded on the principles of the Lord Jesus Christ is in vain and shall not hold. It is important to involve the Lord Jesus Christ in our quest for a rightful life partner. A marriage, which is founded on worldly principles never, gives the couple peace and genuine love. In time it breaks and misery comes in lives of the concerned people. When one is contemplating to get married, he/she is trying to make a lifetime change. To make this very important of all decisions in a life of a person, one must be so careful as to choose the right person to spend the rest of his/her life with.

CHANGE comes with "time."
Therefore Change collaborates with the will of God. That is why when making this very important decision of one's life, there must be Good timing, Judgment and decision. Obviously this tells us something. To make such an important Decision, one must involve the owner of life, who is "time" (Jesus Christ) to move his/her intentions.

CHANGE will never be POSITIVE if one does not involve the king of glory, Jesus Christ. If your marriage was done without the involvement of the owner of "time" who is Jesus, I am sure you are facing unnecessary problems here and there. I must be quick to say that you risk losing that marriage because the Jesus who is SAME YESTERDAY, AND TODAY AND FOREVER is absent. If he is in, then the marriage too shall be the same yesterday and today and forever.

AUTOBIOGRAPHY

My name is Wedson Witson Nyirenda and I was born on 23rd November, 1966 in a town called Ndola in the Copperbelt province of Zambia. My father was named Mr. Tenson Kambombo Nyirenda and my mother is called Etras Banda Nyirenda. I am a third born son, in the family. The first born brother is called Stone Nyirenda who resides in Belgium in a town called Roesalare. The second born is our only sister Helen Eunice Nyirenda. The last born Nelson Nyirenda passed on in 1994 after a very short illness.

I am married to Gillian Nyirenda and we have 5 children. Wedson Jr, Dorcas, Melina, Mapalo and Enoch.

I did my primary education at Fibobe Primary school in Ndola before qualifying to Secondary school at Kansenshi High school where I did my grade 8 up until I qualified to grade 10 and left to join my elder brother in Chingola on transfer. I completed my GCE-O-LEVELS at Chingola High School where I obtained a full certificate after passing with good passing marks.

I also hold several local and international coaching

certificates and licenses. Ranging from the German "B" License, Brazilian coaching license, CAF "A" Coaching license and several FIFA High level and Advanced Level coaching certificates. I also hold the UEFA/CAF Meridian Coaching certificates and the Olympic Solidarity coaching certificates.

I am currently still studying for my Master's Degree in International Management with University of Liverpool –Online.

I am a professional soccer coach and former International soccer player who have played football at highest level. I have played for Zambia's most glamourous club Power Dynamoes and won the African Cup Winners Cup which was then called Mandela cup in 1991. I have played for Nchanga Rangers FC, and Kaizer Chiefs FC in South Africa. I have also played for the now defunct club called Hellenic FC. I won so many Gold and silver medals with various clubs as a player.

I am currently a coach at Club Ferroviario da Beira in Mozambique. I have coached several big clubs in Zambia and have turned them into big clubs in African football. In my coaching career I have been blessed with the winning of so many leagues and trophies for many clubs and I have won so many awards as an individual in coaching.

I am a Born Again Christian by Faith and I am a Deacon in the Redeemed Christian Church of God. I have been blessed with the knowledge and wisdom of winning souls for Christ Jesus while doing my coaching job.

I am a Life Coach and a Motivational Speaker.

www.ingramcontent.com/pod-product-compliance
Lightning Source LLC
LaVergne TN
LVHW051200080426
835508LV00021B/2720